T0194238

O F

SADNESS

A N D   O F

PLEASURE

OF
SADNESS
AND OF
PLEASURE

*A
Collection
of Sonnets,
Limericks
and Other
Poems*

RAY OROCCO-JOHN

ARCHWAY
PUBLISHING

Archway Publishing books may be ordered through booksellers or by contacting:

Archway Publishing
1663 Liberty Drive
Bloomington, IN 47403
www.archwaypublishing.com
844-669-3957

ISBN: 978-1-6657-5734-8 (sc)
ISBN: 978-1-6657-5735-5 (e)

Library of Congress Control Number: 2024903955

Print information available on the last page.

Archway Publishing rev. date: 02/27/2024

CONTENTS

BALLADS

THE POEMS

LIMERICKS

FOREWORD

This book is a compilation of poems written over many years. The poems cover comedy, short stories, and topics people discuss in their daily lives. Some are the author's interpretation of biblical scriptures. Others are based on the author's life experience, including events he has witnessed and people he has observed.

Inspired by Shakesperean and Italian Sonnets, the author has written several of his own in various forms.

The author has included some Limericks in this book which he started writing for fun and decided to share for your reading pleasure.

DEDICATION

This book is dedicated to the congregation of St. Matthews United Methodist church in Bowie, Maryland, organizations of all religions seeking amity and understanding between people of all races, creed, and gender, and finally to my dear mother, Gladys who passed away in December 2022.

SONNETS

Sonnets are fourteen-line poems with a variable rhyme scheme. There are many different types of sonnets including the Petrarchan sonnet perfected by Italian poet Petrarch, and the English or Shakespearean sonnet popularized by William Shakespeare and others. They typically contain between nine and eleven syllables per line. There are several types of Sonnets in this book including those mentioned above. Hope you enjoy reading them below.

1. A FLOUNDERED LOVE

I felt quite cold as the days turned colder,
    The chills too severe for my feeble frame.
With summer fading on our love much faster,
    Its sun dimmed with sudden sadness and shame.
Into winter's night, my heart was shattered
    Like its broken glass strewn on somber streets
Where in delight we once walked unaltered
    In a budding love with blended heartbeats.
Too young to fully grasp love's many woes,
    Our love we presumed was sure to endure
But soon perished by perils from our foes;
    Flailed in our floundering love to secure.
I bear conscious guilt for not shielding her
From their meddling and all dangers deter.

2. A MOTHER'S LOVE LETTER

Despite the neighbor's home you did plunder
    And your sundry deeds of disgust and shame,
My love for you would ne'er be asunder;
    A mother's love, all your vices can't tame.
E'en the sun sometimes accedes clouds of dark
    To wander across its celestial face,
And the world would its brightness briefly lack;
    An annoyance, ne'er a lifelong disgrace.
Withal, your sun in a new morn will shine
    With a victorious brilliance on your face.
Murky skies no longer your path assign,
    And straggling clouds, your new life will efface.
God has ne'er condemned a smeared, risen sun,
Neither will I, a budding first-born son.

3. AGING

My well-versed bones and joints are suddenly
    Speaking to me in lilting, louder tunes,
With my hair starring bright as silvery
    Streamers at midnight in their moonlit hues.
A flight of steps now seeming much taller
    Than the dashing, skyward Eifel tower;
Their slow ascent leaves me gasping for air,
    Stunned I scaled these prior with much power.
My mature mind, now its own enemy
    Recalls those specious kindergarten rhymes,
Though I'm not convinced it's a fading me,
    Rather my boredom playing tricky games.
My most treasured memories yet in place
Against transient foes' quest to replace.

4. AN ARGUMENT ON SLAVERY

An argument that has caused a schism
    Is that human bondage has its merit;
    For it gave poor slaves chances, though tacit
To better their ends. This is sophism.
Perhaps we can accede this truism;
    No clear-eyed man will by choice submit
    To misery's pains, save that to transmit
The sheer extent of his narcissism.
Given the choice, sane sapiens will e'er select
    That which furnishes their lives' fulfilment,
        Ne'er chains, despite what says the nihilists.
Perhaps those fine with oppression's effect
    Must suffer its hopelessly harsh treatment,
        But ne'er will since they too are narcissists.

5. BETRAYAL

You often cause anger, despair, distress,
    Leave a tortuous trail of shock, loss, and grief.
    Your friends in awe, victims in disbelief;
Their backs scarred by daggers you did impress.
You contaminate the minds of the strong,
    Strip them of dignity, self-confidence.
    The young robbed of their future eminence,
Engage in crime with their conscience far-flung.
Doctors, pastors, parents -- your enablers
    Like Judas should experience the cursed tree,
        A fitting fare for their role in your ascent.
Robbing the world of trust, its fruitful years,
    Your deceit renders brilliant minds unfree,
        Bound in a dark path of lasting descent.

6. BLIND VENGEANCE

The light went out on our love abruptly,
    Her snide stabs and trauma taken their toll.
Like a mechanized line in a butchery,
    She stripped all flesh off my solid will.
Dismayed by ensuing pain and anger,
    Selfishly, and fiendishly wished she died.
Ties with forgiveness my mind did sever,
    Trysting with evil, her demise I prayed.
Then found out I, she was bound on her bed,
    And felt much sorrow for her sad struggles.
Regretting all my evil prayers said,
    I asked God, though in vain for miracles.
Of these states of mind -- mercy, and vengeance,
Evermore, will I choose the state of grace.

7. BOUND BY THEIR LOVE

Perhaps ne'er would I see joy in this plight,
  Peaceful rest besides in this humble house
With these fine ladies in perpetual fight,
  Insecure, seeking my life to oppress.
Though despising in much deed each other,
  Do agree to agonize me with pain.
My interest they yearn, my mind to bother;
  One by my toil, the other to complain.
Asks succeeding tasks insisted by one,
  Desire for more pleasure, the other rails
And I bound between these twain loves of mine,
  Hug my weary heart and pray ne'er it fails.
Vague on their plans, but hoping for much luck,
With a lass and a spouse, I'm surely stuck.

8. BULLIES

They can be as plain as old cobblers' shoes,
  Or sometimes, polished like refined gold.
Lacking empathy, caring not for rules,
  Dominance they seek whenever they could.
Classmates, workmates, and siblings are targets
  Of their wretched abuse and sheer terror,
For what they seek, they grab without regrets
  In cold hearted display they're superior.
But for the law, these folks could wreck the land
  With distress, loathing, their will to harass,
And mimics may emerge to join their band,
  Since their victims do oft give them a pass.
Oft a harsh rebuke from a fearsome foe
Is the apt response to their willful woe.

9. HE IS QUITE THE MYSTERY

My beloved brother is quite the mystery;
    His displays of occasional brilliance
In a morass of mediocrity,
    Shocks and chagrins soothsayers in a trounce.
Like flash of light, one would wish a capture
    Of his rare genius can be effectual,
Perhaps in freeing the world from fracture
    Or confirm cures to ills incurable.
In truth, a few are good, and why baffling
    Are his frequent fibs and dopey deeds,
False thoughts and focus on things much footling
    Like his chafing chatter on worthless weeds.
Seems his rare bursts of brilliance aren't just luck
Yet, in his weird world, he might be quite stuck.

10. HER IMPRUDENCE

Her eyes much brighter than the morning sun,
    Her heart bequeathed with nice gardens of love.
    If charm's tall as skies, hers is miles above,
Her sheer elegance, any being would stun.
Her organ fruitless like the bare desert
    Yet, this was ne'er her unique circumstance,
    Perhaps a quite imprudent comeuppance
For she'd squandered that of her was a part.
Neath her gorgeous façade, a heart distressed
    By the permanence of her act unwise,
        Since tried but failed had doctors in this town.
She cares daily for kids crushed and oppressed,
    Remaking them whole, her love she applies,
        Regrettably, none would e'er be her own.

11. HER PARADOX

Her puzzling persona is rather rare;
    She is quite gorgeous, but lacks discretion,
    Very graceful, but fibs with much passion,
Unburdened, like a careless cadaver.
Like a shock-jock, she fills the listening air
    With fabrications to gain attention
    As if her grace and beauty proportion
Is much insufficient for her full fare.
An adulterer that loves to hold court,
    She confounds the mind how the creator
        Could be flawless and flawed in a person.
Even Solomon's wisdom would fall short
    Untangling mess by this dubious suitor,
        Perhaps her grace being the whelming reason.

12. HER PERVERSION

I found out in quite unusual manner
    That you were available, seeking again.
Saw your profile on a dating banner
    Flashed on Mac screen of neighbor on a plane.
Said you were loving, patient, love travel,
    Despise drama, loyal, kind, trustworthy.
Thought you could've been more on the level,
    Yet, preferred your pretty pictures; classy.
Though I could not read all about the dame,
    Shy of being caught spying on the neighbor,
Knew it was false, you skillfully scammed me,
    Perhaps with a new heart, deserve favor.
In seeking the one who'll be true to you,
Being honest yourself would most promote you.

13. HER PLEA FOR LIFE

Piles of dead literally covered the earth,
    Falling densely, some could hardly find room
On valleys, plains, and each plausible path
    To rest their bodies broken by the doom.
Meanwhile, she sat at a lonely table,
    Hoping man like a reconciling groom
Would take a bold step that would enable
    His renewed commitment to better loving.
As the sun ebbed, the moon grew unstable,
    Like the moon, man prolonged his war waging.
With weapons glistening in the wan moonlight,
    She cried for regard with voice now breaking,
"I'm your freedom from all feuding and fight",
But ignored by men yet to see the light.

14. HIS IMPRINT

Chatted with my dad at the brook basin
    About a man who is now dead and gone.
Had a son, but rejected his own kin
    For reasons still unknown, not even one.
He deserted his young household years ago
    Like a thief, leaving imprints at the scene.
Full of himself, the bottle was his foe,
    Soon he was broke, in tatters, pale and lean.
His son offered help, but he turned it down,
    Perhaps feeling guilty of the neglect
He showed the kid who became a baron;
    Successful, rich, the son he did reject.
Before dying, he called his son, "please hurry",
But was too late to say he was sorry.

15. HIS OBSESSION

Last night, I saw you lazing by the Lake
    With his sinful arms around your shoulder.
Watching you two was like biting brick cake,
    Love he may, but mine for you is bolder.
Last week, I peeped you half-dressed, reading,
    And kept watch until you were safe asleep,
Then saw you spit chewing gum while walking
    And grabbed it; a souvenir for my keep.
Trailed your taxi till you were safe at work,
    Petted your puppy when it jumped the fence,
Sent nameless posh gifts to your office desk
    And watched true beauty exposed while you rinse.
He can't dote and adore you like I do,
And never will go where I will for you.

16. INTERRUPTIONS

She pokes her nose in all forms of man's life
    Being around e'er this fragile world was formed.
E'en Adam did adjust when his dear wife
    Introduced her in Eden's floral ground.
Guilty she is oft of undue meddling,
    Though some of her timely acts maintain man.
Her sudden presence may lead one doubting
    God, the maker's firm contingency plan.
She may bring brief laughter to sad mourning,
    Swiftly cease a cute couple's wedded bliss,
Bring startling snow to a balmy morning,
    Or simply barge in while shy lovers kiss.
She hasn't palpable plans to change her ways,
So, mankind must contend with her always.

17. Life Without War

A thought suggested which I find silly
    States that life sans war is impossible.
I can't disagree more with this theory
    For it means fights make man's life possible.
Though war could be a means to mankind's end,
    It's just one of his wide ranging choices
With no hard condition that it be tabbed
    In lieu of measures from peaceful sources.
In contrast, man has e'er been capable
    Of quite thriving living without warfare,
Excepting those periods, he was unable
    To deter greed and grudge for his welfare.
To think life sans war is impossible
Rob's man of peace and all he is able.

18. Me at the Fork

Here at the fork with no aspiration
    To camouflage my life's bungled romance.
Strange that I with requisite cognition,
    Succumbed those wanton acts of dissonance.
Not one minute for melancholy strain,
    Sad regret or stumbles in self-pity.
Granted new path likely dotted with pain,
    Can tread no more, that of insanity.
Will shun bright butterflies morphing to wasps,
    Seeming innocuous while raiding my tent
Or cute lady bugs aping lethal asps
    Whose superficial hugs could leave me spent.
Love's treks are complete with more goading roads,
Hence, I wouldn't tread those with allure's vile loads.

19. MY BURDEN

I killed a man who once pillaged my home
    Trying to end this tranquil life of mine.
Had him and I but met before this shame,
    Could've paid for his work, his ethos refine.
Although he may have been to wrath confined,
    Could I have pleaded with him to disarm?
Conversely, I did twice, but he declined.
    Why did Him above not prevent this harm?
Now, I live with breaking His sacred law
    And all the greater with a broken heart.
He was someone's dearest, despite his flaw,
    I bear the pain of tearing them apart.
Would I feel the same if his gun hadn't missed?
Couldn't really tell since I would be deceased.

20. MY REGRET

Wish I hadn't broken many doting hearts
    By making fancied demands of their love
To appease my unappeasable wants
    Yet, like a boor, kept my love in a cave.
This loneliness that's ravaging my heart
    Like a deluged dam does my life engulf,
Perhaps a just reward for my conceit;
    Not long lasting I hope, it has been rough.
Had unpeaceful stints of sleepless nights
    On hollow bed as quiet as a grave
And lonely trips to resorts and concerts;
    All my afflictions, I truly deserve.
Love, pray for you and chance at redemption,
With a bowed head asking your compassion.

21. MY TRAVELS WITH HIM

As we strolled down our street, I was much touched
    By his graceful struts when we turned the bend.
Many tough years together we've journeyed,
    Yet we're still going strong; he's a dear friend.
He's thrilled when suited with new rubber shoes,
    Though cold mornings do make him quite cranky.
He purrs while we pick up radio talk shows,
    And craves organic juice which makes him happy.
Through some harsh years, he's been quite resilient;
    Each shock life has presented, he's absorbed,
Shielded us from strong winds, heavy fog, sleet,
    Slips and slides by those neighbors who flailed.
Once, he spent days rehabbing his bruises,
But he's back for us to go on cruises.

22. MY WRETCHED CROSS

Quite heavy my heart is tilling this ground,
    In thrall of the man, I see no clear end.
No rest for recall, none with whom to bond
    But a beast with wooden cross I call friend.
He bears his cross weary with my grief,
    Slogs on at my command to move the earth.
He knows that him nor I will see relief,
    Since neither of us had chosen this path.
Down on one knee, writhing in pain, he cried,
    Hinting he's done! His form can no more trudge.
Then fell he heavy on the earth and died,
    Me whipped for his loss by the man of drudge.
This sad experience does place in my mind,
My cross before me, and my friend behind.

23. NEAR THE OPEN SEA

In a wistful walk home by the seashore,
    I observed winds and waves pound the broad beach
With greater vigor than I'd seen before;
    Would they be bothered by my eyes' wide reach?
As waves fall though rising high and mighty,
    Days are brief, since dark clouds cloak the sunlight;
Leaves sensing graveness succumb gravity,
    Weakened and wind-swept on my lonely route.
With rusting skin, they're strewn by the wayside
    Like those I dearly love but now are gone.
A loyal few stay much closer beside
    As we enter the front door of my home.
Others must be spreading news about me;
"Alone and without, near the open sea".

24. NO BASIS FOR SELF-EXTINCTION

Those we loved along life's perilous way,
    Who once like us were hopeful of what may,
Yet by their own hands took to cloudless day,
    Made us heedful about this life's brief stay.
We can't presume their mind's predilection
    But must conclude much torment was endured,
To cease what the maker in cognition
    Of their joyful comfort, kindly endowed.
Life, precious than things in its allotment
    Mustn't be sundered at mortals' self-pleasure.
Perhaps swap setback with new engagement,
    Then from sad failure, bounce back with leisure.
Despite this life's numerous strain and stress,
There's no basis for man's early self-recess.

25. NO IS ALSO AN OPTION

Slaving at others' dreams is never good
    If your drudgery somehow defers your plan.
While you provide their precious needs like food,
    Their dependency will your life constrain.
Quite frequently will they return for alms,
    Notwithstanding your need or fond desire.
When in their failures you express your qualms,
    With vengeance at you, your life set afire.
Never be selfish, yet don't be suckered
    By melancholy shows; their fishing bait.
Your bliss need not be teary-eyed, puckered
    As unwitting accomplice in their plot.
Offer help as much as your heart will do,
Yet "no" is sometimes all that you can do.

26. NO ONE SHOULD IN KIND REPAY

Tis said that no one should in kind repay
    The wicked done to them by their neighbor
Yet, this wisdom oft counters man's reply
    To seek justice and quell hurts they harbor.
So, here lies man's quite cumbrous conundrum;
    He mustn't have the heart of a callous boor,
By virtue, apt to counter his outcome
    Yet, expected to ignore when assailed.
To withstand floods of abuse and succumb
    Against man's innate habits is harebrained,
Since man has been shielding from the onset.
    Perhaps insist none cause harm or be harmed
Purging any instance of man's upset,
Then you'll get his best since there isn't a threat.

27. ONE PART STILL YEARNING

One part still yearning for her, says I must,
    The other opposed, insists I must not.
Their coin toss vetoed by my mind whose trust
    Was betrayed by her; it says, "trust her not".
We were birds that flew in the summer time
    When the skies were blue, and our sun was hot.
As one, we sang love songs in time and rhyme
    But like the sun, our music reigned and waned.
This twain of my heart strikes me like a chime
    And though there is conflict, not much has changed;
My heart, she's quite cunningly split apart,
    My mind, conscious yet of her acts deranged.
One heart in two parts and one mind alert
Will sadly ne'er more be of her a part.

28. OUR WEDDING NIGHT

Late that night, after our wedding party,
    Slipped in room she'd darkened with wall paper,
To break that for which my wait was lengthy;
    Her declared chasteness which was my fetter.
Howling as though stricken by labor pain,
    She expressed anguish I aroused on her;
An awful husband somehow a villain
    Was through rather quickly after much heat.
Then peeped the morning sun through the curtain,
    Exposing the ichor splattered bedsheet.
Said it was shed when her membrane broke
    Yet, none on me or her, except dried sweat.
I baulked as the wily, feigned maiden spoke,
Then the headless cat was found by her folk.

29. PEOPLE WITH PURE JOY

I can't for those rare people with pure joy
    Concede any roadblock. Joy is treasured
Only by those privileged with true joy;
    It does not falter e'en when disrupted.
Joy is truly joy when the joyful share
    That which is most vital to their wellbeing.
Man's thriving isn't likely, absent the care
    And regard for joy's place in good living.
Joy isn't commonplace, but must be nurtured
    By hearts with place for joy and placed above
Everything. Joy points past its well natured
    Self to man's pure nature and will to live.
In true joy, souls are exposed to sense joy.
If wrong, prove I am by first sensing joy.

30. POINTLESS PERFECTION

My folks took no less than pure perfection
    Sadly, in all I said, believed or did.
Oft, when I erred or made an omission,
    Rebuke was swift, for these they did forbid.
Through the years, I for this perfection strive
    Which in no time evolved my obsession
And did my daily human dealings drive;
    Finding flaws became my mad profession.
Though this hopeless practice brought some success,
    It mechanized my mind, stripped me of heart.
Wish I had shed this stupid, pointless mess
    For my sake and for those I did upset.
If you should dare obsess over all things,
Be fit for the strings and heartaches it brings.

31. Stolen Happiness and Dignity

What makes a brother subject some people
    To cruel hate and worthless fate by stealing
That which was bequeathed by God, the noble
    For their delight, to lavish his longing?
Suppressing in steady steps, he managed
    To make those people the means to better
A clan. In a race biased world, inflamed
    This wickedness by lynching to foster
Fear and loathing. This unfairness, grievous
    And vile, stripped from those people their divine
Days. His greedy allies though quite conscious,
    Stood still to stop evil, since they were fine.
Their silence signaled consent for control
O'er other folks and was a wretched role.

32. The Agony of Sloth

They are strong, wholesome men and women, free
    From life's stresses, yet don't do much it seems
    To give of their best and avail their means,
But oft celebrate their state with much glee.
These that sit idly by will for e'er be
    Enemies of time and likewise their dreams,
    For in killing time, they therefore their dreams,
Yet this concern, their minds can't clearly see.
These oft have pretexts for any failure,
    For bereft they are of any commitment,
        And chafe at challenges to their status.
Not applying their aptitude is sure
    To curb the altitude of their content.
        Like it or not, this burdens all of us.

33. THE BED

An old man in the village once declared
    That the comfort folks get from a night's sleep
Depends on how well their bed is prepared;
    Unclear, but his words were thoughtful and deep.
Your business partners could break your neck
    If treated poorly; they are your pillows.
Colleagues against you could stack the deck
    Like a mattress; always massage their egos.
Your attitude like those sheets on your bed
    Can be abrasive or smooth; the latter
Brings sweet dreams with no worries in your head,
    The former, bruises that'll make you scutter.
Make your bed to comfort the worst stranger,
You will sleep well without fear of danger.

34. THE FACES OF FATHERLESS KIDS

In the abyss of distress and despair,
    The fair faces of weak, defenseless lads
      Dimmed as their full sun was cloaked by dark clouds
Shrouding their hopes, bold dreams, and future care.
Ne'er their set circumstance, parents in pair
    Littered them while the sun flashed bright arrays,
    Yet, the foolish man took to the byways
And like the clouds, his deeds were quite unfair;
Brief ties with guileless lads he did sever,
    Leaving lives saddled with shame and sadness,
      Cared not for their pain and unsure future.
Their dimmed faces will stay with me ever,
    I need not reach afar for their likeness,
      But stare rather clearly at the mirror.

35. The Sitter

For years, she prudently looked after me,
    Mom worked nights, dad as usual, not around.
One cool night she said, "just sit down, let me",
    With a wry smile, sat on me -- my hands bound.
Her jingling lobes against my guileless face,
    My eyes cleared like his in Eden's Garden.
Thoughts of my folks' failings quickly erase,
    She'd stirred my dreams, blotted out my burden.
Later apart, yet now and then together,
    On her wedding eve, sat on me again.
My folks can ne'er repay their debt to her;
    She was my pleasure, their absence much pain.
Before you judge me, you must consider,
My folks found her for their lonely toddler.

36. The Truth

The earth was foolproof with your firm, pure hand;
    Your rightness like a clock's hour hand is sure.
Earth lost her virtue when fibs stormed the land
    Like maiden broken without her pleasure.
In you, life has been right through joys and tears;
    Dispensed fair justice by your even hand,
Yet being accosted in your advanced years
    By those furthering a false, deceitful brand.
Unclog the minds of people in your midst;
    Children, parents, and pastors when they preach,
Judges, teachers, and lovers in their tryst,
    And politicians, so your facts won't breach.
You've been absolute about things you say,
Send a clear message, you are here to stay.

37. THEIR NEGLECT

I'm grateful for seeing this life's chapter,
    Where e'en brute lions with cubs affection share.
'Twas not my choice when they knew each other;
    Partnering pea and pod, they brought me here.
Rightfully, I should be sheltered, clothed, fed,
    Enlightened, but in essence, dearly loved.
The mob-like hostility they've displayed
    Convulses a heart which was unclouded.
I'm often blamed for their selfish address;
    Neglecting my needs, she buys her good looks,
He is mistress bound, while son in distress,
    Grandma is great but they are more like mooks.
With a sad heart, I ask their attention,
And sliver of their love and affection.

38. THEIR PREDICAMENT

In a distant land was quite a skilled man
    Whose aptitude kept his quaint town alive.
Far and near they came for this oppidan
    To heal their diseases, and to survive.
On a cold day with steeple bells pealing,
    He was marched through town in somber ritual
For exile, with his stunned partner trailing
    In parade of shame that was unusual.
Lucky he'd escaped summary execution
    By callous town elders of high esteem,
Who'd damned him for defiant deviation
    For he'd fallen in love with one like him.
He was soon asked back when some children died;
Absent his skills, minds had been enlightened.

39. TO SAVE THE TOWN

Early on, father made clear I was different
    From my brazen brothers who of pale skin
Were ne'er restrained in his quite apparent
    Quest to steer the town to their sordid gain.
While toiled I in foul fields through rain and sun,
    They slowly learned from the well-learned in town,
Then fiddled I at night balls for their fun
    And ran errands from the fields to downtown.
As days daily drew my drudgery harder,
    Launched then I fervent protests on my fate.
But he hugged me saying, "not to bother,
    To save the town, I had to acclimate".
Ne'er being a learned man, quite thrilled was I,
But in sooth, he meant my worst woes were nigh.

40. WHAT SHE SEES IN HIM

His appearance is nothing like the sun,
    Upset it would if were to him compare.
The Ogre more pleasing peeks than he'd gain;
    If teeth be wreath, dead wreath his mouth did bare.
Her grace belies her attraction to him,
    His brutish ways besmirches her bright star,
Befuddling the mind, what she sees in him,
    Besotted by him, he wreaked harm on her.
This beast conned his way to her lonely heart;
    With parents gone, she'd craved companionship.
Friends haven't prevailed at keeping them apart,
    Now she lies in ward wrestling with a drip.
The law has promised to mete him justice,
But would she yet love him just as he is?

41. WORDS HAVE GREAT POWER

Guilt-stricken once reading my factual prose,
    They inquire if it's written about them,
Not seeking truth, but mainly to oppose,
    They disparage, distract, curse, and condemn.
One cried, "why not mention I attend church,
    And provide my dear son's necessities.
Focus not on my few failures as much,
    But my actions' many affirmatives".
Facts, steadfast e'er the world was formed,
    Could ne'er be altered by a simple prose.
Perhaps practice they these facts -- whate'er learned
    Seeking to amend their lives, ne'er the prose.
Words like science breakthroughs can effect change.
Done appeasing, I'll write all in my range.

42. WORLDWIDE DISPARITY

The world appears racing to the bottom,
    The mighty force the weak to foot the bill,
Knocking them down like glum leaves in autumn
    By sapping supplies and stifling their will.
Some lands distressed with not enough to eat,
    Dark days, sad cries as hungry children sleep,
Yet others, lavished with waste in repeat;
    Wealth as vast as dividing oceans deep.
With their warring weapons of crude terror,
    Subjugate the landscape, strut their soiled wealth
Through grim horror, heedless to their error,
    Steering a fragile world to failing health.
Unless the world sees each other as one,
Disputes will arise, its demise is done.

43. YOUR STARS' FADING LIGHT

Summer shivered at your scenic splendor;
    Bright silver bells, evergreens, and spangles
Drove her to distress and hopeless horror,
    Unlike you, she interests not my fondness.
On my knees, shared a ring in December,
    But my heartful deed was erased in waste.
Father died on sad day I remember,
    Upending plans with you to celebrate.
I still trust you, and hope you love me too,
    But the sun stays lit than your stars lately.
Carols, candles, wreaths my spirit renew,
    And I nothing lack when you show fealty.
Loved you e'er since childhood, need not enshroud,
But shine your star lights hidden in the cloud.

BALLADS

44. MY FAIR MAIDEN

My fair maiden is quite rare to be real,
    With our clasped hands we'd show fond affection
As we stroll the city streets where we'd feel
    The stare of friends stunned at love's devotion.
This bee couldn't match his bud's perfection,
    Yet her love's great and I'm blissfully blessed
For her heart -- a bastion of compassion,
    Shares my burdens, hence I'm ne'er depressed.
Days aren't days sans her sunny complexion,
    Her nighttime absence obliterates rest.
Our long stares stirs heaven's celebration,
    Tis then our love like the sun shines brightest.

45. THERE'S NO MORE TO DO

Gradually growing old and decrepit,
    I look back with fond, but mixed emotions
Bemoaning those prospects missed quite a bit,
    Pondering how I botched those interactions.
Stood atop my delightful days with passions
    Hotter than the summer sun at midday,
With maiden gardens in many sections
    Wishing to bear me a lovely bouquet.
Acted a fool in my vacillations,
    Keeping many a doting heart at bay.
With the sun setting on my ambitions,
    There's no more than done so far, that I may.

THE POEMS

1. A Fine Blessing Reserved for All

1. A fine blessing reserved for all
     On splendid, cloudless day.
   Many do long for this honor,
     Love's lack holds hearts at bay.

2. Maids it oft requires and bearers,
     Parents, and friends and guests,
   Mitered parsons or justices
     Affirm lovers' requests.

3. He steady, stands at the ready
     For a peerless princess,
   To unveil her with a fond kiss
     At proceeding's recess.

4. Such graceful, willing assistants
     Meeting their every call.
   The fine pair sharing bright spotlight
     While waltzing at the ball.

5. Cheerful this special moment is
     For all with zeal to feel
   Love's exhilarating passion,
     From time eternal's will.

6. Yearning this choice, selfless day is
     Never, never too late.
   This prime day, pretty preordained
     Is engraved in one's fate.

2. A Harmonious Place

1. On a nearby land rests a group
   In harmony and quite sanguine.
   Solipsists thrive not in this troupe,
   Since hearts are pure and genuine.

2. Here, hate and fear are much eschewed;
   'Tis one for all and all for one,
   Hot teas of ire are never brewed,
   Nor desires grabbed at tub of gun.

3. Here, acts aren't callous or fatuous;
   Its folks reflect the common good,
   Never are they crass or fractious
   Even in this mélange's worst mood.

4. One man's bad break animates all
   To comfort their beset comrade.
   Fares of accord are prepped for all
   To calmly dine and be assured.

5. Folks don't each one manipulate,
   Assured hearts abrogate this need.
   There isn't cause to prevaricate,
   Their innate hearts are true indeed.

6. Indeed, this haven quite sublime
   Might be too much to ask of man,
   Yet, lived I here, in dreams of mine,
   So too in sooth, could any man.

3. A HELPING HAND

1. Though he was not my dad by birth,
       He sure aided my rise;
    From toddler trips through puberty,
       Kindly in fond reprise.

2. Babies stumbled at their first steps
       Guided by mum and dad,
    Until they learned to lean on legs
       Without the aid applied.

3. And teachers frame those fragile minds
       Of pupils in their care,
    With patience that the maker hands
       To those that care to share.

4. You know how it feels to hold one;
       Its warmth enough to calm
    The chill of being alone asea
       With no assist or balm.

5. We have all held a helpful one
       From strangers, kin, and friend.
    Hence, ne'er demur with one to lend
       Whene'er it's in demand.

4. A Most Amazing Son

1. A most amazing son,
       Who on the cross was hung;
       My sin to purge, and right the wrong
   That Eden's curse begun.

2. Beside him, there was none,
       The father's trust was strong;
       Who'd shed his blood and not prolong
   My days and nights of mourn.

3. His cross the veil has torn
   To everlasting dawn
       And saints no more to death belong,
       That heav'n can claim its throng.

4. His oust of Satan done,
   My helplessness is gone;
       I dare not to my sin return,
       That bridge to heaven burn.

5. His consequential turn,
       The task did not impugn
   But shared his love and did not shun
       The pain of Calv'ry's thorn.

6. A most amazing son
       On Christmas day was born,
   Rose with the resurrection sun
       That early Easter morn.

5. A Rich Man

1. His house was full of wine and gold,
   His pow'r more than a king could hold.
      His spread of wealth speaks the story
      Of his life and mortal glory.

2. Stay here today, there tomorrow,
   Much of his life sees no sorrow.
      His unchaste mind could hardly rest
      Since fast females were oft his guest.

3. Yet at last, the Lord, God did send
   His perverse pleasures to its end;
      At his parting, not e'en a friend
      Was there, nor mourning lilies found.

4. On that day, the earth sore and vexed,
   A downpour from on high obtained;
      His cup was full, his vault deluged,
      In sooth, he could not be entombed.

5. Hence, friends be wary that riches
   May buy you gold, earthly niches,
      Yet, God's true word is all you need;
      Plant in your hearts, salvation's seed.

6. ALL MY GIFTS FOR YOU

1. In service of your holy will,
   I will work valiantly until
   All your tasks on this earth fulfill,
   And in mankind your love instill.
   > To your holy work aspire,
   > All my passion, my desire.

2. Earthly treasures; silver and gold,
   Not an ounce, would I e'er withhold.
   Sharing my gifts, your love uphold,
   Bringing your children in the fold.
   > All the means that you have giv'n,
   > All I have is yours in heav'n.

3. In your obeisance, bend my knee
   Praying your spirit falls on me,
   Like the Lord implored on the tree
   And died to save me full and free.
   > All my fervent pleas assured,
   > All my life in you procured.

4. In all my thinking, make me pure,
   Sanctify me from the allure
   Of the world's vile ways that obscure
   The mind, and your blessed work detour.
   > All my heart to you I give,
   > All I am, where'er I live.

5. My life and all my granted skill,
   I'll humbly use, your tasks fulfill.
   Pilot me while I climb the hill
   Assuring peace and your goodwill.
   > All my gifts your will to do,
   > All my talents, e'er for you.

7. ALIVE THROUGH GRACE

1. Man was dead in his transgression;
   Sinful ways were his blight,
   Bound in doomed regression.
   Aping Satan's disobedience;
   Pain and strife, day and night,
   Were his inconvenience.

2. Like the rest, man was by nature
   Full of grief, often wrong,
   Facing Satan's torture.
   God made man with Christ the union;
   In his pow'r, pure and strong,
   Man in God's communion.

3. By his grace, our souls he's saving,
   Not by works, none can boast
   That they are deserving.
   All our needs his love supplying;
   One by one, at no cost,
   Man his grace receiving.

4. God raised man with Christ in heaven
   By his grace, man was saved,
   Through his faith in action.
   Pow'r that God has shown in meekness;
   Mercy on the depraved,
   Perfect in his weakness.

5. Now with him in heaven resting,
   Saints on high in their glow
   With angels attesting
   That our God so full of mercy
   Will provide, here below,
   Grace to men unworthy.

8. America, The Bright Shining Light

1. America is at her best
   When vast, encompassing her nest
      Of scintillating minds;
   Where optimistic souls are bred,
   Their tribalistic instincts shed
      And much success abounds.

2. Her ships and finest armament
   And aircraft in her firmament
      Are not her most adored;
   What the esteeming nations see,
   Desire is her democracy,
      Without, her light's deformed.

3. Her stunning gleam that makes her great
   Has sundry sparkles in each state
      Who pool their minds as one;
   They come from all around the earth
   To share their talents, art, and mirth
      Which shimmer like the sun.

4. Yes, there were times she saw dark days
   With slavery, spite, and social frays
      Engaged in wayward ways;
   Sometimes those days dragged on to years,
   Subjected tribes to trail of tears
      Which stained her radiant rays.

5. Yet frequently she did not rest
   Against vile tyrants in their quest
     To persecute the meek;
   She freed Jews, Muslims, Germans too
   Through sacrifice and strength anew,
     Her gleam redeemed the weak.

6. Every new step of faith she takes,
   New ground of light and truth she breaks
     While trusting in her God.
   Her burdens she will overcome,
   And kindred spirits will draw from,
     To shine e'er bright and bold.

7. No other one upon this sphere
   Who welcomes all that have desire
     To reach their dreams, but her.
   Although her vision sometimes blurred,
   Her light shines on for greater good.
     God bless America!

9. BIRDS OF A FEATHER

1. Tis said that birds of a feather
      Often communally would flock.
   Hence, one would be quite shocked to see
      A dove palling around a hawk.

2. What if bird alike in his quest
      To relieve the hawk's predation
   Decides to befriend, to cajole,
      And provide proper direction?

3. He can't randomly from afar
      Think worst of the mercenary
   But have to experience firsthand,
      Depth of its moral quandary.

4. He would need to appreciate
      It's motive for rapacity;
   For hunting the weak and humble,
      And penchant for atrocity.

5. Like him, all persons must refrain
      From stating guilt by alliance
   On those hanging with the world's worst
      Hoping to convey clearer sense.

6. Birds of a feather flock as one
      Often, becoming quite the pest.
   The same may have someone with heart
      Unlike the much-detested rest.

10. CAN I STAND WITH HIM APART?

1. Can I stand with him apart?
   Can I purge my selfish heart?
   Often wanting, seldom give,
   Fear of losing all I have.
   Til in you I fully depend,
   I'll be empty til the end.

2. Those I dearly love are gone,
   All I am is skin and bone.
   Friends may pledge their love and care
   Yet, their troth is far from dear.
   Til in you I fully depend,
   I'll be empty til the end.

3. Struggles deep that overwhelm,
   Leave me yearning for some calm.
   Dreadful days that turn to nights,
   Sleepless stirring, endless frights.
   Til in you I fully depend,
   I'll be empty til the end.

4. Doubts that dominate the mind,
   Fears that cast me in a bind
   Cause my heart to overflow
   With a sadness, harsh and slow.
   Til in you I fully depend,
   I'll be empty til the end.

5. I know coming days are bright,
   I can see your shining light.
   In my struggles, shed my doubts,
   Worries, wants and sinful bouts.
   Teach me Lord to trust your word,
   Then I'll be full til the end.

11. COMING TOGETHER

1. What's wrong with us in this world we belong
   That we can't simply get along?
        We have greatly harmed humanity;
   With pow'r and greed pertly subjugated
   Sisters, brothers to those acts detested,
   Suffering yet from slavery perpetrated
        By condoning vile supremacy.

2. How long shall we survive those dreadful acts
   With malice and hatred impacts?
        We have seemingly lost our minds;
   Our neighborhoods are quite separated
   By race and class, cruelly segregated,
   Yet often claim no one is prevented
        From the aspirations of our lands.

3. Why give up on peaceful ways to end strife
   And bring much meaning to this life?
        All nations would need to consider;
   Trading bombs for things not detonated,
   Mediation to solve things disputed,
   Restoring lands to persons uprooted.
        These must be a part of their charter.

4. When will we agree precious lives are worth
   Our time and toil for full rebirth?
        We must all take on this tall order;
   Prejudice must ne'er be tolerated,
   Just justice should not be complicated,
   To truest ideals, must be committed,
        Bringing inhabitants together.

5. Which of us will always welcome the throng,
    Building nests in which all belong?
        We must do our very best to try;
    Know each other since we are related,
    Disagree, but savor what's accepted,
    Ensure wealth isn't singly concentrated,
        Hence, all men get a piece of the pie.

12. Deadly Sins

1. Lord, I was pride; could not embrace
      Meekness and virtue, you inspire.
      Lured and beguiled by self-desire,
   Yet saved by your redeeming grace.

2. Lord, I was greed; I could not give
      Others, the things to me you blest.
      Now, your blessings bring out my best
   And tells this sinner share and live.

3. Lord, I was sloth; could not employ
      Talents you lent me for your work.
      Now, you've granted my life the spark;
   My zeal inspiring love and joy.

4. Lord, I was wrath; I could not cease
      Crudeness that rouses ire and strife.
      But your pure spirit calmed my life,
   My mind from mindless rage release.

5. Lord I was lust; I could not keep
      My heart from envy, I confess.
      But you did save, forgave my mess,
   And kept me far from Satan's heap.

6. Lord, you have cleansed me of my stains;
      Pride, wrath, greed, and sloth no more mine.
      My lustful heart you did refine,
   And rid me of those deadly sins.

13. DEATH OF RACISM

1. Generations witnessed your dreadful act
    Enjoined, benefitted, and played a part,
    Adamantly, man will own this error
    And rid himself forever, your terror.
    Your bell shall toll on that fateful day
    Yet, with no pomp, none will dare to say
    Your name aloud, or your departing mourn.
    No tribute your blind bigotry bemoan,
    No notables gracing this gloomy ball,
    Or e'en the lesser of men bearing pall.
    No demented chorales singing your praise,
    Or drunken mourners each their voices raise.
    No mad weather gods your fate decide,
    Or mitered nobles in tow preside.

2. Just loving hearts as one celebrating
    Fairness, inclusion; each other building.
    On this day, man himself and by himself,
    Blind to color, rank, and class will excel
    With a pure heart and a mind at ease
    Will see in himself how good he is.
    He will share with him that has a need,
    To union and fairness, plant a seed.
    Dole out equal and principled justice;
    Unbiased, fair, and kindlier as just is.
    And you, erased from his heart at last
    Along with rest of your hateful past
    Shall be interred with the goons in hades,
    E'er a shining world enjoy gentler shades.

14. DEPEND ON GOD

1. We strive hard and expect to prevail,
   Long days and nights, all to no avail.
   Then, question the Lord, Jesus,
   Why should it happen to us?

2. We trust our careless courage and might,
   Make vague promises without foresight,
   Fight for pow'r, yet we discuss,
   Why did it happen to us?

3. Shattered dreams and broken promises,
   Worthless pow'r, stricken by diseases,
   Man must e'er depend on God;
   Lost he is without His word.

15. EPITAPH FOR A BELIEVER

But for these rough, broken stones,
You will feel no more troubles.
You've left a sad, fallen world
As a true believer should;
Conscious, with eyes quite clear,
His name on your brows you bear.

16. Epitaph for a Fun Musician

He lies here decomposing
While stones stand firm opposing.
He rests not from his labors
But from basses and tenors,
Wishing for that trumpet sound,
Else here e'er in this place, bound.

17. Epitaph for a Teacher

Here lies the brain of students
Beneath these stones of prudence,
Without his, theirs are hopeless
With minds of great stock, witless.
Withal he shall ne'er instruct
And no one will e'er obstruct.

18. Fellowship of Believers

1. If the world could truly devote
    Its time and effort to promote
        Teachings of our dear Lord;
    Boosting its love and fellowship,
    Sharing with true companionship,
        Twill be in one accord.

2. It'll be in awe of our great God,
    Since he has always kept his word;
        The world in joy as one.
    Many would sell prized possessions,
    Share their gifts and make provisions
        For the weak and the lone.

3. Each day, they'll gladly assemble,
    Confer and differences settle,
        Break bread with each other.
    Opening doors to friend and neighbor,
    Sharing love, affection, favor
        As sister or brother.

4. Hearts will oft be true and sincere,
    Praising God, his promise revere,
        Loving life's good pleasure.
    They'll receive everlasting peace
    From him who makes all wars to cease
        And provides good leisure.

5. A world without God surely will
    Hate sustain, and mindlessly kill
        The very souls it needs.
    If one only sees the other
    As enemy, not a brother,
        Ever, the world recedes.

19. FORGIVENESS IS A BALM

1. He took boys in from out the street
    Into his mansion huge and neat
        To share in his fortune.
    The three poor lads were suffering,
    Spent days and nights out wandering;
        'Twas their only option.

2. They quickly took to their new life,
    A far cry from their time of strife
        Near an inspection post.
    But soon their greedy spirits struck,
    Caused them to lie, defraud and trick
        Their benevolent host.

3. The three were caught after they tried
    To pledge the treasure they had pried
        From mansion of their host.
    They ended in the cellar dark,
    For they, the township's laws did break,
        Bail they would need to post.

4. Then suddenly their host appeared
    To bail them out the jail confined,
        And took them home again.
    In rueful tears they pondered why
    Their host would common sense defy;
        How could his trust regain?

5. Then they inquired why he had shown
   A rare and selfless love unknown
       In spite of their deceit.
   He then replied that he was giv'n
   Chances to fail and be forgiv'n;
       His life was the receipt.

6. Thereon, they lived under his roof,
   Saw much success and were the proof
       Forgiveness is a balm;
   Two boys turned doctors, one a cop,
   The host indeed became their pop,
       Their lives constantly calm.

20. FURTHER I RUN AWAY FROM HIM

1. Further I run away from him,
   The closer he would get.
   My oft farewells to loved ones show
   How frequently we've met.

2. I saw him grab the neighbor's pal,
   His son, nephew, and niece,
   And caught him swipe a smart, sweet girl
   From her mom's warm embrace.

3. I was quite helpless as he clutched
   A baby down with him,
   Lucky, in sooth he did not act;
   This time was just a dream.

4. On my last birthday, struck again,
   That time, my brother's wife;
   I cried and pined in awful pain
   But was told, "such is life".

5. It seems no one is shielded sure
   From his oft wretched quest
   To rent relations into shreds,
   Even when at their best.

6. I will confront him on his stride
   With prayer in this strife,
   Whene'er by him from earth be pried,
   So be it, such is life.

21. GOD'S BLESSINGS

1. God with blessings on man can shower
   In spite of status, class, or power,
   Not on the merit of his deeds
   Or the immenseness of his needs.
   God will bless as he sees fit,
   No one his purpose can defeat.

2. Ne'er be envious of those he endows;
   Fullness of neighbors, friends he allows.
   In execution of his will
   And with a promise to fulfill,
   God can bless as he desires
   Those he loves, and he admires.

3. The world may think some don't deserve
   Blessings he pours from his reserve.
   Who is man to question the love
   Which he shares from heaven above?
   God can bless abundantly,
   Frequently and suddenly.

4. Blessed is man who trusts in God
   And with him be in one accord.
   All his detractors shall be shamed,
   Those who oppose him be disgraced.
   All his life shall be at ease,
   God will bless him with his peace.

5. Pray then that soon you may enjoy
   Grants in your life, he will employ.
   May he take pleasure in your ways
   That on his face, your eyes may gaze.
   God will bless with all you desire,
   You'd never want and never tire.

22. HAVE FAITH THEY SAY IN TROUBLED TIMES

1. Have faith they say in troubled times,
       Be hopeful and be strong,
    But sadly, fail to clarify
       How to, and for how long.

2. How would they know unless they've been
       Afflicted or in pain?
    Where hopelessness and doubt appeared
       To torture and to reign.

3. Strength is much overcharged it seems
       As to our faith's concern.
    Enduring pain and fading strength,
       Patience can overturn.

4. And for how long our faith can hold,
       Must lasting hope depend.
    The evidence of things unseen
       Must quicker time transcend.

23. HE THAT SEEKS WHAT IS RIGHT

1. He that always seeks what is right,
      Heart is pure, never cheats,
   Acting aptly in God's sight;
   Genuflecting ne'er to idols,
      Daft mistakes ne'er repeats,
   Spends no day with scoundrels.

2. He'll ne'er spoil a neighbor's partner,
      Nor see one, not his own,
   God's good grace he would garner.
   Doesn't oppress the weak and helpless,
      But returns pledge for loan,
   His life will be blameless.

3. He won't perpetrate a robbery,
      Shares his gifts with the rest;
   Feed the poor and hungry.
   To the naked, he gives clothing,
      Gladly gives of his best.
   Those near him lack nothing.

4. He won't lend his wealth at usury
      With a scheme to defraud;
   Stealing from God's treasury.
   He'll withhold his hands from evil
      And his will, bold and good
   Will repel the devil.

5. His days will be ever golden
      Following God's decree,
   To his will beholden.
   Judge his peers rightly and fairly,
      In God's eyes, favor see,
   He will thrive assuredly.

24. HER DEVIOUS HEART

1. Her deviousness was evident from the start,
   And for a while kept us farther apart
   >Yet, I trusted her in spite of my doubt;
   Was aware of her penchant for lying,
   Oft, she feigned love by simply crying,
   Money, she found much more alluring,
   >But convinced myself things will work out.

2. Her thirst for quick wealth and fine material things
   Could not be quenched by a thousand wellsprings,
   >And at last reached a point of no return;
   Stifled by stagg'ring debt, she was drowning,
   Amass more debt by more borrowing,
   Clothes ne'er sufficient for her wearing,
   >Her greed raged like fire eager to burn.

3. My role as mate was to keep us together
   So, I did my best to always please her.
   >But she had other haunting things to do;
   Relied on other's awful counseling,
   Convinced her looks were for pursuing,
   Said was with me, yet was two-timing,
   >And declared it was her time to go.

4. Before she left, was eager to clear her mind;
   A display of her vile, superficial brand.
   >Staring at me, let it all out, saying;
   She was with me, not that she was loving,
   But for things, I was not providing,
   Pressed me for cash for her departing.
   >I said good-bye and started praying.

5. So, then she left but soon wanted back inside;
   Found the grass not as green on the outside,
       I vowed to keep our attachment erstwhile;
   Her unsettled love, now overwhelming,
   Her many canards now disheveling,
   Her tactics no more persuading,
       I spurned her attempts to reconcile.

6. I should not have tried at such a devious heart
   Horrible as she was right from the start,
       And to this day engages in deceit;
   I blame my imprudent heart for trying
   To gain love that wasn't for my winning;
   An act that brought me close to dying,
       For hers was a vile heart of conceit.

25. HER FACADE

1. I always wondered why my mum
     Would never speak her mind.
   In spite of how my dad behaved,
     She never was unkind.

2. With all his disingenuous ways,
     She'd always keep her word.
   The senseless things that he would do,
     Her voice was never heard.

3. She'd always wear a smiling face
     Though deep down she was sad,
   But never let her kids find out
     That things were really bad.

4. She'd always keep her solemn vow,
     "For better or for worse",
   But one can see she never got
     Dad's best, just his perverse.

5. Her selfless show of love extends
     Beyond our dwelling's walls;
   She would his love-child's life sustain
     When he declined the calls.

6. Some selfless souls do find their hearts
     Attached to loveless mates.
   Their sunny disposition oft
     Belies their damning fates.

26. HIS JEALOUS MIND

1. There was once a bitter and struggling man,
   Mad at the world and without a good plan.
       Surpassed by thriving friends and family,
       He spent time, oft dejected and lonely.

2. He went early to his garden at eight
   To pick some produce for his dinner plate,
       And there he met the Lord, God the spirit,
       Ready to bless him, though he lacked merit.

3. I have seen your struggle, the spirit spoke,
   I have blessed your dear friends and all your folk.
       Consider, I'm the God of the living,
       Ask your humble wish, it shall be given.

4. The man quickly thought and said, I demand
   That with your vast command, you would remand,
       The success of friends, and folks I despise,
       So, they are poorer than they realize.

5. I'm sick of their pleasures, he persisted,
   Show off their wealth, act like they are gifted,
       I'm certain, they are no better than me,
       Make them my equal, so their faults they see.

6. Like flash of lightning, the spirit was gone,
   Shocked by the jealousy the man had shown,
       And the missed prospect to receive the aid
       From him who alone can lessen his load.

7. 'Tis sad how resentment makes us unkind
   When spiteful emotions hijack the mind,
       And miss out on the blessings God promised
       To the hurt, humble, struggling, and dismissed.

27. HYMN OF LOVE

1. God of immeasurable love,
   Send down your spirit like a dove,
       The longing hearts to bind;
   Give love to all your humankind,
   For you are merciful and kind
       With blessings unassigned.

2. How great your love on us bestow,
   All broken hearts you will restore
       And grant us love at last.
   But until then we'll never feel
   The love endowed with holy zeal,
       Unless you cleanse our past.

3. So, hope and faith and love we see
   But, yet the finest of these three,
       Indeed, the best is love.
   Remove from minds our hate and stress
   And let our hearts to you confess;
       Create in us true love.

4. The loveless things that we embrace,
   And spiteful spirits you'll efface
       To make us love again.
   Then make our loving hearts aspire
   That with your spirit we'll conspire;
       Your confidence regain.

5. Your son, his love in full display,
   In selflessness his life did lay
       And all our sins forgiv'n.
   Make us like him to freely give,
   In love and mercy ever live
       Like saints with you in heav'n.

28. I Am Not One to Care for Luck

1. I am not one to care for luck,
    It never walks my way.
   No matter what its boosters say,
    My mind, it does not sway.

2. It often seems much overcharged
    Like green on apple tree;
   Its promises that often fail,
    Hard work does guarantee.

3. Now and then, it may boast success
    And pleasures from its ruse,
   In fact, it is man's hard progress
    That ushered in good news.

4. One's overhyped import of it
    Discredits the maker,
   Who doles out gifts as he sees fit
    To credit the taker.

5. I'll stick with working hard each day
    And keep an even keel,
   If it by chance wanders my way,
    It won't change how I feel.

29. I'M SURE THAT SHE EXISTS

1. I'm sure that she exists
        Despite my fickle heart,
    Her love will keep my eyes awake
        Until we're ne'er apart.

2. I'm sure she'll understand
        Since I've been ne'er ideal,
    When she sets out my deeds to pry
        And hence to seal the deal.

3. If only I could change
        My incoherent ways,
    She'd soon appear in image clear
        To fortify my days.

4. I'm certain she exists,
        For in my dreams I've seen
    All that her silent love has writ
        In places where I've been.

30. I Remember Giving You My All

1. I remember giving my all;
        Gazing at your fair face each day,
    Brightened when heaven's shining ball
        Like our love was in its hay day.

2. I remember you had made plans;
        Cold hearted, much unknown to me,
    Brought vile birds in our humble nest,
        Played me a cheap pawn in your game.

3. I remember my cheeks were drenched
        In creeks of pain you ushered in,
    Flowing straight from your thoughtless heart
        Oblivious of my grief within.

4. I remember the words you said,
        "You'd rather die than show me love".
    Left me scars from your horrid ways,
        The best of minds could not remove.

5. I remember finding out he
        Left you cold for one of his dames,
    Seeing how well he had gulled you
        Like you did me in your sad games.

6. Now you'd like my mind to erase
        Memories so awful, yet true.
    I'll live out all my coming days
        Joyous and fruitful without you.

31. It Floods the Fields, Fills Every Path

1. It floods the fields, fills every path
   And ubiquitous in the earth
       Like clouds dotting the sky.
   It scales the mountains, walks the plains,
   Treks breadth and length of bloody veins
       Like flour in bread of rye.

2. The human body knows it well,
   The mouth and hands and ears can tell
       It's nigh e'en while asleep;
   The ear, melody while it sings,
   Heart sighs when much relief it brings.
       The eyes though, not a peep.

3. It wrestles with the raging sea,
   Grants lift to those wishing to see
       What lies beyond the skies.
   Restocks the athlete with new zeal
   And stays with those severely ill
       Until their last goodbyes.

4. It gives life to a fading fire,
   A yawn to working men who tire
       And sustains storks on high.
   Though seemingly aloof, listless,
   Its omnipresence is doubtless,
       Cold or warm, it is nigh.

32. It Seeps from Bloated Womb

1. It seeps from bloated womb
      Conceived in the azure.
   Its heft the layer agitates,
      So, earth its flows assure.

2. It flies through open space,
      Slides down a slippery slope.
   It visits tombs, green nurseries
      And all within its scope.

3. It lashes roofs and walls,
      Wild beasts and people too.
   All those who dare stand in its way,
      It slashes like a hew.

4. It dashes farmers' hopes
      With crops submerged in field,
   Though it delivers joy and cheer
      When a parched soil is stilled.

5. It blasts the earth often
      Carving a mountain path,
   For streams or rivers to be born,
      And sustained by its wrath.

6. It shades the forests green,
      Nurtures the plains of wheat.
   It replenishes humankind
      Suff'ring the sun's defeat.

7. It reaches oceans wide,
      Succumbs the sizzling sun,
   Then vanishes the naked eye
      And to its womb return.

33. It Was a Sham

1. They've been together many years
     With kids now fully grown.
   The flawless living oft portrayed
     By them, disproves what's known.

2. She's kept a love interest awhile
     To counter his neglect,
   And the many trysts he has had
     Which showed his disrespect.

3. Their marriage sham later became
     Unmistakably clear;
   He leaned to lust and ditched his wife;
     One more became his dear.

4. One could then look beyond their mess
     Since all on earth have erred,
   But he was pastor of a church
     Whose life ought not be stained.

5. Sham marriages are sure to err
     For they are acts in vain.
   Their lack of an emotive bond
     Routinely makes it plain.

34. Jesus, My Utmost Power

1. Why should I fret the vast unknown,
   Or what this sinful world has shown
   When Jesus is my trust alone?

2. Close ties and those I love may fail
   And envious pals my plans derail,
   But Jesus will his aid avail.

3. God's tasks none other can equate;
   I find myself inadequate,
   But Jesus will my life dictate.

4. The world in terror may distress;
   My confidence, and drive depress,
   But Jesus will my life redress.

5. Though Satan tempts me every hour,
   My joy and cheer seeks to devour,
   But Jesus is my utmost power.

6. Though I may fail his tasks fulfill,
   I know he cares and loves me still;
   Jesus, my confidence refill.

7. Though faint and troubled, sore, oppressed,
   I will remain forever blessed,
   Since Jesus is my hope and rest.

8. I pray my ears would hear his call;
   Him who is true, my heart enthrall,
   Jesus; my life, my all in all.

35. LIFE'S SPINNING WHEEL

1. I think of those rare, dear days past,
     When round and round and round I went
   With no worries to rant about,
     And not a cent I spent.

2. Then I saw how in silence they
     Toiled hard and tried to foot the bill,
   For all my varied needs, and then
     Wished my days will stay still.

3. But soon dear days to decades turned,
     And here and near and there I went
   With much to do and merely earned
     Enough to pay my rent.

4. So, 'twas my time to do as they;
     Spent I, and spared not e'en a cent
   To bring my offspring all that's due
     For needs such as a tent.

5. Life's spinning wheel will ne'er relent,
     Goes round and round; spend and be spent,
   E'en when apart from earth be rent,
     The next man shall be sent.

36. LITTLE BIRDS FLY THE LANDSCAPE O'ER

1. Little birds fly the landscape o'er
        Foraging for shelter,
    Food and drink to escape the dire
        Man's moral disaster.

2. Flying from tree branch to cliff's edge
        For that inviting nest,
    Sway in the wind like periled sedge
        Without its soil to rest.

3. Their feckless folk hide in plain sight,
        Unmoved by sad failure
    To care for offspring, trapped in blight,
        And fruitful lives assure.

4. Like burdened Atlas, fly around,
        Damned by their folk's neglect.
    'Twas not their choice to be earth bound
        To suffer and be wrecked.

5. The folks can make cute little birds,
        But these birds can't make folk
    Care for their young, stringing strong cords
        To take away their yoke.

37. LOVE FOREVER

1. Once I pined in weary sadness
    For a love, that was strong,
    Then you brought me gladness.
    Life without you I can't fathom;
    Empty days, dull and long,
    Just another phantom.

2. Once my heart was lost and lonely
    And I was, in retreat,
    Scared of loveless phony.
    Then I met you like none other;
    Heart so pure, kind, and sweet,
    Gives me not a bother.

3. When I think of us, I ponder
    That my life, which was dull,
    Now in blissful wonder.
    All the while my love is yearning
    For your smile, or your call
    Daily, brightly shining.

4. Now my gleeful heart rejoices
    For your love, warm and dear,
    Best of all the choices.
    Keeps me happy, always singing
    Everywhere, loud, and clear,
    You, my joy are bringing.

5. You my dear, I'll always cherish,
    Live for you, for I know
    Our love will ne'er perish.
    Hostile winds will try to sever,
    But our love, in its glow
    Will be here forever.

38. Love's Loneliness

1. I think about her each day and night,
   Hoping against hope she feels the same;
   That in her sweet dreams, cries out my name,
   And likes my likeness in her blurred sight.

2. She broke our romance not long ago;
   Seven weeks, three days to be exact.
   I hope that her skewed script can redact
   The rash judgment made on my ego.

3. Tis said, falling in love's a blessing
   Whether doting hearts valiantly fail,
   And sad, nagging grief triggers their wail;
   Such sentiments don't my pain lessen.

4. Now, she strolls my street with her new man,
   Callous to my love, her actions show
   Love's loneliness with its anguish slow,
   For she's stuck in my mind and my plan.

39. Man is Like Seed

1. Man is like seed a farmer sows,
   His life depends on where he grows,
       Pray that he has good soil.
   He will be tested, tempted oft
   And evil taunts must not corrupt;
       The devil's plan must foil.

2. Those who would fall along the path
   Where treads the multitude of wrath,
       Vile birds will soon devour.
   Like flash of lightning, they depart,
   Remembered not in any part,
       Their root will ne'er flower.

3. Those who would fall on rocky sod
   Will quickly spring with shallow mud,
       Yet in the sun will fade.
   Whose labor toils in helplessness
   And withers fast in hopelessness,
       Their frail root will abrade.

4. Others will fall among the thorns,
   Then swiftly grow in wealth and moans
       And suddenly recede.
   Whose uprightness they abdicate,
   Ensnare in sin and suffocate,
       Their root will not succeed.

5. Yet others fall on soil that's good,
   Creating fruit, a hundred-fold,
       Never see days of gloom.
   Their root is the almighty's word
   And watered by the spirit's flood,
       In righteousness they bloom.

40. MOTHERS

1. They are our keepers from of old,
   The safeguard of the family.
   Some can be as precious as gold,
   Others can be downright silly.

2. They can be sweet, gentle, caring,
   Kind, quite forgiving and charming.
   They'll stay up late into the night
   Til the children turn off the light.

3. Some can be reckless and selfish,
   Annoying, mean, and abusive.
   Others can be brash and bullish,
   Wild, bad-tempered, and possessive.

4. Mothers can feel the awful pain
   Of their wild child's ill-gotten gain.
   Bow their heads in prayer between
   For the Lord, God to intervene.

5. Mothers can be loose, adulterous,
   Yet, hope their kids will be virtuous.
   Some neglect their children's nurture
   Yet, convinced they're sure to be pure.

6. You can tell mothers your secret
   And be sure it'll remain discreet.
   From them you can get compassion,
   Be drenched in love and affection.

7. Some skip their innocent childhood
    Prematurely to motherhood,
    Only to find their enticement
    Results in utter resentment.

8. To this end, we may reason
    And give everyone her due.
    All good mothers are women,
    The reverse is not so true.

41. MUST I?

1. Must I for sinful parent be
       A distressed, restless soul?
       My heart his many deeds console,
   His blood availed for me.

2. Must I fearing vile men refuse
       To do my maker's will?
   No clever lie or good excuse
       Any my task fulfill.

3. Must I for love of self embrace
       The devil's vile design?
   Then will I fall flat on my face,
       To helplessness confine.

4. For on that day when he shall call,
       Then I must ready be,
   Or soar to his eternal hall
       Without the crown on me.

42. MY DEAR WIFE'S GARDEN

1. My dear wife's garden was well stocked
     With ecstasies and much beauty
   That truly had dear Eden's trounced,
     And humbled e'en when it's moody.

2. Often, I got to feel its warmth,
     Whether the air be hot or cold,
   And spritely sprinkled its parched earth
     When she required, or as I could.

3. Yet, her primed plot failed in blooming,
     No matter what or when I did;
   E'en my prim trees and shrub trimming
     To lift its seeming sterile lid.

4. Then found out I that she had prepped
     Her garden soil as she'd desired.
   In spite of all my sprinkles sprayed,
     No chance my blossoms would have bloomed.

5. Her deceit left me much at bay,
     Watching open maiden gardens
   With wish to bear me bright bouquet,
     Without a trick or sham burdens.

43. MY VALENTINE

1. Somewhere in the garden is a fine rose
    Whose sweet smell draws me very close.
    I wish to find that lovely flower
    That upon me its dear love may dower.

2. Like a butterfly each blossom I search
    To find the one that's the best match.
    A task not easy, but worth taking,
    A trip full of thrills and compromising.

3. In this hearty hustle for the right mate,
    I'm reminded of a great thought;
    That all good things come to those who wait
    And with you, I know it is not too late.

4. Hence, at risk of boring you with my task,
    Thought that you'll allow me to ask
    Like young lovers, since the turn of time,
    Will you dear lady be my Valentine?

44. No More Tears This Christmastime

1. No more tears this Christmastime,
   Enough was shed throughout the year.
   Time to be near those people dear
   With love that will efface all fear,
   Bringing joyful cheer, loud and clear.

2. No more fights this Christmastime,
   They've brought much restlessness at night.
   Time for us to restore what's right
   With peace that shines as bright as light
   Bringing calm to a world in blight.

3. No more gloom this Christmastime,
   It has for long our lives consume.
   In full bliss, time for us to bloom
   With clearer minds that can make room
   For the one who'd end our dark doom.

4. No more hate this Christmastime,
   It's stained the world with shame and crime.
   Let choirs sing and jolly bells chime
   With hale hearts as one, and sublime
   In love and peace this Christmastime.

45. NOTHING TO WORRY ABOUT

1. God's my shield above my shoulders,
   Lifts me up above all others.
       When I call, he answers prayers,
       I'm not concerned with fears and cares.

2. I try hard not to flout his laws,
   If I do, he forgives my flaws.
       When I plead for grace, compassion,
       Never had I a rejection.

3. Now and then, foes rise against me,
   Thinking he would not defend me,
       But I'm saved by the God I serve
       And my foes flee at his resolve.

4. Foes attack me on every side,
   I fear not! In God I reside.
       He is this man's sure deliv'rance,
       Who's blessed with his abundance.

46. OF SADNESS AND OF PLEASURE

1. Of sadness and of pleasure,
   Our dear charming cheeks adorn;
   The glad glees in good measure,
   Yet, quite painful for they that mourn.

2. For the eye, a cleansing flow,
   The mind, a burden dispersed.
   For the soul, an obvious show
   Of numberless feelings suppressed.

3. Proving that we are human,
   And care for selves and others;
   They relieve, man or woman,
   And refresh much more than showers.

4. They are mankind's emotion
   For loving hearts' devotion,
   Be it times of elation,
   Or bitter days of dejection.

5. Trickling or quite outpouring,
   Running or mist-like dropping,
   Throat closing or eye welling,
   Or unshed, they are quite telling.

6. Hence, in your joys and your pain
   Lasting through the coming years,
   Remember, there's nothing vain
   In plain displays of love and fears.

47. ON OUR WAY TO PARADISE PEAKS

1. Fellow at the helm gave his orders,
       His cohorts did their safety checks,
   A right, left, right, a sudden pause
       And were off to Paradise Peaks.

2. My knees shaking and heart pounding,
       Both palms sodden in nervous sweat,
   Coiled my weakened legs to ensure
       I was pressed firm against my seat.

3. I grabbed the rails or so I thought,
       It was the neighbor's icy hand.
   Staring at me, frightened like me,
       He was surely one of the band.

4. When we were at terrible tilt,
       My heart jumped out its firm casing.
   Only my stiffness pushed it back;
       My breathing tight as unyielding.

5. As we reached heaven's entry port,
       A sudden calm began to form;
   The clouds below like safety nets
       Returned my body to its norm.

6. Fellow at the helm spoke again,
       This time of obstacles ahead.
   Wished he had kept this to himself,
       Cause my head was full of much dread.

7. Boom! an obstacle from the right,
   Clang! one more plunged us to a tilt.
   A boy cried as we approached town,
   While I grabbed for a life at wilt.

8. I shut my teary eyes to pray
   And empathized with birds aloft.
   Then perceived I why wise Emu
   Marches home every day and night.

9. I was relieved at our next stop,
   Some unmoved by the sways and dips
   But like Emu, I'm now convinced;
   Hence, I'll walk to Paradise Peaks.

48. OUR LOVE

1. O dear! You've giv'n so much to me;
        Affection, care, and love.
    That which our hearts and minds agree
        Was made by God above.

2. Was it for things that I have done,
        Your love for me has grown?
    I count my blessings one by one,
        Your light on me was shone.

3. Each time I see your lovely face,
        My joyous heart's afire.
    This fortuitousness embrace,
        You're all that I desire.

4. To see how well our love has fared,
        Your heart, a search might need.
    The warmth and beauty I have touched
        Is all that one would read.

5. So, even could one see your heart,
        It would show nothing new.
    I give myself to you, sweetheart,
        'Tis all that I can do.

6. And when our earthly days are done,
        We will to heaven soar.
    Be with our maker on and on,
        Our perfect love to share.

49. PARENTAL LOVE

1. I wish my parents had been taught
   Their duties for the child they brought
       Into this world to live.
   Displayed their pride in selfishness,
   Dereliction and foolishness,
       No eyes could dare believe.

2. When things were bad, I was between
   Their rage, resentment always seen
       And oft would face their wrath;
   She would in anger call him names,
   With spite he played his many games,
       I was in their warpath.

3. My heart in pain and loneliness
   Could not experience happiness;
       Peace, nowhere to be found.
   I often mused of such a place
   With love that would my pain erase,
       Where joyful lives abound.

4. In escalation, there was tort,
   Their lawyers played who was at fault;
       My custody to solve.
   Went to and fro between the two
   And met the sad homewreckers too;
       Is this parental love?

5. My mother hurt was not herself,
   She often saw in me, himself
          And took it out on me.
   My father's drunkenness was clear,
   When he was sober, seldom near
          To take me out to sea.

6. Then suddenly he ran away
   Unto a country faraway,
          I was too young to cry;
   How can he claim to be my pop,
   Yet makes a kid and flies the coop?
          Not even say, "goodbye".

7. Of all the things children must have
   With peace and joy for them to thrive
          Is pure parental love.
   No gifts or clothing can replace
   Abuse, neglect children can face.
          Therefore, show them true love.

50. PERHAPS I AM NOT GOOD ENOUGH

1. Perhaps I am not good enough
      In all I've done or do;
   Had cold rebuffs and feedback rough
      As soles on this man's shoe.

2. I sang their church songs loud and bold
      With much emotions bared.
   They claimed I went quite overboard,
      As if the maker cared.

3. At work, I oft outdo my size
      On tasks and exercise.
   As blind as bats, they criticize
      For me being too precise.

4. My verses give them fits it seems;
      Too plain is their pretense,
   Yet, complicated often means
      Literary death sentence.

5. I seldom reap those benefits
      Of gifts bestowed by man,
   The maker knows as he befits
      Blessings in this life's span.

6. Yes, I may not be good enough
      In man's marred view of me.
   I'll take a chance, however tough
      On the maker's decree.

51. Prayer for Mercy

1. You set me apart, your faithful servant,
   I call your name when distress is torrent,
   You grant relief, yet I often stumble,
   So, to you Lord I pray, meek and humble;
   Have mercy on me and hear my prayer.

2. When sin is rampant, I am faltering,
   My restless, throbbing heart is wandering,
   I offer sacrifice of righteousness,
   And humbly repent, for my wickedness.
   Have mercy on me and hear my prayer.

3. Some people turn your splendor into shame
   By trusting their vast wealth and fleeting fame.
   When they repent and seek your forgiveness,
   Honor your word, acknowledge your goodness.
   Have mercy on them and hear their prayer.

4. Deranged thoughts overwhelm your own people
   Whose actions fail to be wise and humble;
   Seeking false gods to fulfill their desires,
   Yet call on you when their error backfires.
   Have mercy on us and hear our prayer.

5. You, O God will bring us prosperity,
   For your light will shine on us more brightly.
   Fill us with joy, though we may have little,
   Keep your people safe when spirits are brittle.
   Have mercy on us and hear our prayer.

52. SEPARATED, BUT NOT THEIR LOVE

1. He was her soul mate at first sight,
   In love, yet disengaged
   By regulations of their land
   Through monarchies endorsed.

2. He was a peasant's only son
   But she was royalty.
   His mum serving as palace cook
   Displayed her loyalty.

3. She first saw him on palace grounds
   When mum brought him to work,
   And instantly their lives became
   Of love, not just a spark.

4. By rule, the two cannot be mates;
   Their classes contravene.
   They dodged and kept their love discreet
   And let God intervene.

5. They married each a partner, yet
   They were so much in love.
   Nightly, their portraits bid goodbye
   With tears flowing thereof.

6. Though far apart in others' arms,
   Their love had much resolve.
   Unhappy were their marriages,
   Whose ties did soon dissolve.

7. Thereon, they moved away from home
   To circumvent the laws.
   And tied the knot as they had wished,
   Blooming in endless bliss.

53. SHE ZEROED IN ON HER DISGUST

1. She zeroed in on her disgust
      With him; distressed he'd not
    Done just as he'd promised, and she
      Said, "it was all for naught".

2. She sat at the table alone
      Bemoaning his harsh tone
    When he'd spoken. This meal it seems
      Will be only for one.

3. He returned home with a fine pair
      But she owned these shoes too,
    Among others she'd bought and hence
      Does not have need for two.

4. On his third try, he thought nothing
      About the product's price,
    But wanting to please her, he checked
      Not once, or twice but thrice.

5. Was met by his pet on fours when
      He returned, hoping for
    Better reception from his wife,
      Who'd waited since hour four.

6. He gave her the pentagon shaped
      Band, and she came alive;
    It was just what she'd hoped for, so
      He got hugs and high-five.

54. Sometimes I'm Saddened Not Because

1. Sometimes I'm saddened not because
        Of things I need or rare ailment,
   But by mean deeds of those I love
        Who ne'er seem quite content.

2. Give them the best of all you have
        In food, clothing, cash, and comfort,
   And suffer yet the worst of man
        From souls whom you support.

3. Stuck in sea of greed and offered
        Generous means to stay afloat,
   They'd rather submerge and perish
        With their boatload of loot.

4. If you should refuse their requests,
        Be ready for their wretched wrath,
   For it worries them not how oft
        You've helped them tread that path.

5. Perhaps 'twas meant to be this way
        For those covetous and unkind;
   E'en founts of philanthropy can't
        Quench their philistine mind.

55. Tasted a Fare Never Prepared

1. Tasted a fare never prepared
   From silver crafted fish.
   The best saucier in the world
   Can't create such a dish.

2. Gluttoned of evergreens, I'd stay
   And lustful of fresh snow.
   Thinking through holly holidays
   On which parties to go.

3. When gift shops cringe at rare requests
   By patrons and their corps,
   When church chorales' sweet carols cease,
   I shall binge even more.

4. When tinsels, bows, and sparkling wreaths
   Are wrenched from homes and trees,
   When pealing bells from steeples stop,
   I'll feast in high degrees.

5. Till the man comes in bright red suit
   With his midgets in tow
   To gaze this gormandized wobbler
   Kissing neath mistletoe.

56. TEARS OF GOOD-BYE

1. I rarely hear the words good-bye
       Without a pause or tear.
   This was ne'er my set circumstance
       Until a recent year.

2. Before, these words were casual speech
       With all I hoped to see
   Again, whenever time permits,
       Wherever that may be.

3. But this was altered when she spoke
       These words and slept away.
   I wish our parting kiss had been
       Enough to make her stay.

4. Hence, ne'er do I these words presume,
       My heart, they always tug;
   A tear, her sweet remembrance shed,
       A pause for lasting hug.

57. TELL OF THE MASTER

1. Where the Lord seeks you, his parson be
     Are distant lands cloaked in darkness' veil;
     With scriptures rare, and the children wail,
   Say to the master; here am I, send me.

2. Reach out through all the desolate nave
     Where hunger is rife, and fights prevail,
     Yet, none know of him that cannot fail;
   Tell of the master; only he can save.

3. In troubled times, through Satan's outburst,
     Nighttime seems long and the laughter rare,
     Yet daylight welcomes fresh joy and cheer!
   Glory in the master "Thou art the Christ".

4. When subject to the vile heathen's shame
     For sake of the savior, faithfully,
     Though all may seem lost, pray peacefully
   Unto the master "Hallowed be thy name".

5. Look to his throne in heaven above
     For that flawless mate, your equal yoke.
     Bless you he will, his love must evoke,
   Singing of the master "Our God is love".

6. In your loss or grief, and life's turmoil,
     Recall who alone has all the might
     To comfort and calm where there is blight,
   Believe in the master for he can heal.

58. The Church is in Dark Delusion

1. The church is in dark delusion,
      Though Jesus Christ is Lord.
    Through vile schisms and dissention,
      She blesses those with sword;
    Enabling mean wars and menace
      Against the savior's will
    For all to live in joy and peace,
      Their precious lives fulfil.

2. Mid sad scenes of human conflict,
      She straddles the sidelines.
    In untold prejudice affect,
      She sought cordial confines.
    Her courage darkened by this fact;
      She's drifted much astray
    From that which the Lord did instruct
      To keep watch and to pray.

3. In bed with king and emperor,
      Their influence she craves.
    While weak natives die of hunger,
      Her affluence makes waves.
    She has in time all forgotten
      Her purpose as laid out
    By Him, the only begotten,
      To save the poor and lout.

4. In grief and utter suffering,
      Sad natives dwell with dread,
    Her silence ever deafening,
      Their blood, the tyrants shed.

She mocks His unsparing passion
    And dreadful agony,
For all to be in communion
    In peace and harmony.

5. In trysts with many a despot,
    She's stained her radiant ray,
Darkened like the once dreadful spot
    That shrouded Calvary.
Her light for all, ever His dream
    Yet, her eyes marred to see.
Her temple once unveiled by Him,
    Now cloaked in secrecy.

6. To serve the restless natives well,
    She must to scripture turn;
Espouse the faith which clearly tell
    Of the begotten son.
Then shed her recent horrid way,
    Free natives from their pain
And reclaim her once vivid ray
    That she might shine again.

59. THE EMBARRASSMENT OF JEALOUSY

1. Though man's oft consciously aware,
       It could well be disguised
    By his mind quite unconsciously
       With self-reasons devised.

2. It activates not his actions
       To try or work harder,
    But demands he steals or covets
       The best from another.

3. Dependent on man's emotions,
       It'll make him kill humans.
    Joseph turned out to be lucky;
       His life was sold for coins.

4. Tis said it can be good because
       It protects relations;
    I fail to grasp this paradox
       Seeing its warped tensions.

5. It can be a potent motive,
       Subject to one's values.
    Acts must not hinge on passions when
       Faced with poignant issues.

60. THE FALL

1. Starring head and shoulders above all,
   At seven foot-three, a man stands tall,
   But knees buckle, and then a big fall,
   On the ground and out, he is quite small.

2. In the meadow, the rich owns a mall,
   Dwell on the hills and having a ball.
   Suddenly, misfortune makes a call
   That placed the humbled rich in a pall.

3. Somewhere in the tree, the leaf's a stall,
   Strong winds, very heavy rains, and all.
   In winter's cold as bitter as gall,
   The lonely, helpless leaf takes a fall.

4. In the open jungle you'd recall
   The lion wrapping its prey like a ball.
   Yet, small blood-sucking fleas in a squall
   Cause the king of beasts to take a fall.

5. In the battlefield, there is a brawl;
   Brave and scared men, and a fiery wall.
   For cover and help the fallen crawl
   Neath dead bodies bouncing like a ball.

6. For a leaf, the beasts, mankind, and all
   Dwelling on this massive, earthly ball,
   E'en the deadly fleas, however small,
   No one is quite exempt from the fall.

7. But He, the one who heeded the call
   To free mankind from his sin and gall;
   Jesus Christ, prince of heaven and all,
   Only He is ransomed from the fall.

61. THE GREEN FIELDS OF PEACE

1. Once were green fields we used to roam
      With serene scenes, always at ease;
   The sun hugged its flowers and kissed
      Its grain, and all things were at peace.

2. They were green fields with grains like corn
      Which man tilled with much pride and fun.
   As kids, we watched in awe, each morn
      Fresh flowers, trees and shrubs being born.

3. Then they were red fields; air pitch black
      With fine brains like grains strewn around;
   Disposed for being quite predisposed
      To brainless strife while peace abound.

4. Now, they are green fields once again
      Where life and lifelessness agree;
   Coarse grass conjoin dank tombs of man
      Where once were grains and a grape tree.

5. These same green fields, we must now traipse
      With somber gait and sorrow heart;
   Fleeced of innocence, stripped of ease
      By man's desire to tear apart.

6. There will be green fields e'er for man
      With man its love to cultivate,
   Where grains of peace must e'er be strewn
      And love in full bloom resonate.

62. THE IMPERISHABLE

1. Snatched by the reaper on the fall,
    Claiming his fresh bounty.
   My desperate pleas, profound protests
    Were much futility.

2. There was no carriage, bells, or pomp,
    Nor the hat-waving throng.
   He sped through evening dews to place
    With sunny days far-flung.

3. Then set me in a house that scaled,
    Three-wide, by eight by six.
   Enough for me to be obscure
    From the crabby commix.

4. Neath mounded stones -- his stashing spots,
    I heard their angry sound,
   But then the rumbling quieted
    In a quarter less bound.

5. After hour three-score and twelve,
    The trumpet blew the clue;
   My frame in radiant skin, he fussed,
    Was imperishable.

6. The bright winged squadrons of the skies
    Glanced me with joyful eyes,
   Lined dazzling path to greater heights
    Where awaits me the prize.

7. Then reached we o'er the azure plain
    Where sits the trinity;
   The father on his sapphire throne,
    At last, eternity.

63. THE IRONY OF REJECTION

1. I've been rejected many times
        By lovers, jobs, and mates,
    Though each unique in circumstance,
        Their impact raised the stakes.

2. Though awed, she snubbed me for she felt
        I was not right with God,
    Her insult was the driving force
        For me to seek the Lord.

3. Some bosses turned me down for jobs
        For being unqualified,
    Those cold rebuffs supplied the spark
        To enlighten my mind.

4. Friends to whom I was kind and just
        Failed to share love and care.
    Their actions prompted that I must
        Find those with love to share.

5. Life's spurns that oft test one's resolve
        Are part of its grand scheme.
    E'en those that seem shockingly cold
        Bring fortunes yet unseen.

64. THE LEGEND OF TOUGH TIMES

1. He often seems to come my way,
       Wherever I may be.
   With subtle tests and things to say,
       Sometimes too much for me.

2. I would not claim to know his signs
       Despite how oft we've met,
   But this I'm sure; he commits crimes
       On those he has beset.

3. He murders dreams and strips the soul
       Of its security.
   Robs parts of future, hides a goal
       In his captivity.

4. Found out ago that he was bound
       With pal, complexity.
   In twain, tried to impale my mind
       And my dexterity.

5. On special days, approach he would
       With much hostility.
   No strength or planning ever could
       Hold my tranquility.

6. Sometimes they claim he'll soon be gone,
       No solace does this bring;
   For he and pain are tied as one
       When hopeless songs they sing.

65. THE LORD OUR GOD SITS ON HIS THRONE

1. The Lord our God sits on His throne;
    Those other gods, we shall have none,
    And we must worship God alone.

2. The name of God must be revered
    For He is true and dignified,
    And we must show our due regard.

3. Six days we labored, and we pressed,
    The seventh day is for our rest,
    This is the day the Lord has blessed.

4. Parents, guardians we must respect,
    For they are wise and can direct
    Our lives so we are made perfect.

5. For God alone has pow'r to take
    What he has formed in His namesake,
    Killing our own, must ne'er partake.

6. Have no desire to be alone
    In bed with one that's not your own.
    This deed, our God will not condone.

7. Be satisfied with what is yours,
    God cares for needs, and opens doors,
    So, steal not what your neighbor stores.

8. When faced with choice of truth or lie,
    Always speak truth and don't deny
    A neighbor's justice or their cry.

9.   We must not crave a neighbor's wife,
     Such passions are with danger rife
     And God abhors them in this life.

10. Do not be envious of your friend,
     Or ever let your greed upend
     The blessings, God for you intend.

66. THE RED RIVER

1. By the cliff stood a red river,
   The sight of which makes one shiver.
   It flowed the blood of conquered men
   Tossed by enemy now and then.

2. For here had raged the fiercest fight
   By men who could not see the light.
   Bodies battered and hopes shattered
   By vain wars, reckless and scattered.

3. For what could mankind really gain
   From causing each other such pain.
   Destroy the life God has spared us
   For a world that's made us callous.

4. For here men had shed precious blood
   Into the river, deep and broad.
   Hope against hope to beat the flood
   Of grave barrage and endless brood.

5. This river calls to mind the one
   That flowed Christ's blood on calvary.
   With Satan's conquest fully done,
   It was an awesome chivalry.

6. His blood can cleanse all men who plunge
   In his river; pure, deep, and wide,
   Which can all stains and guilt expunge,
   And welcomes sinners; come, abide.

67. THE SALIENCE OF MUSIC

1. There isn't one like it in the world
     That primes the brain for things
   We do, sending chills through our spines
     As awed, enraptured beings.

2. It can change gloomy moods without
     An assist from a pill,
   And e'en renew a fainting heart
     With zeal and guide its will.

3. Without exception, all cultures
     Make it a part of life,
   Although its pulse, pace, type, and theme
     Are with distinctions rife.

4. Oft, it requires a stick wielding
     Director on a bus,
   Where all aboard know well the speed,
     Dynamics, flats and stops.

5. Minsters could lose their soul partner
     If of it are deprived,
   Praising the maker will be stripped
     Of passions it derived.

6. God bless those who bring it to us,
     Whose gifts we presuppose,
   And those who did, but now are gone
     To rest and decompose.

68. THE SANITY GARDEN

1. He is not like the despondent dud at home,
    His silhouette covers this luscious flora dome
    Flushed with blue bells and daffodils bursting,
    The blue capped chaffinch, and wrens warbling.
    And he is soft and gentle with a warmth I desire
    But, here by nature's work, not mine to aspire.

2. This place! O this place; such calm, such beauty,
    Far cry from lonely palace of pain and duty
    Where I, ostensibly confined, for better or worse
    To a mate's whims and moods; my illustrious curse.
    Here I feel wanted, nature always singing praise,
    In toasting to bliss, its tulips like glasses raise.

3. The place is alive with fluttering butterflies
    Gracefully gliding over bright lovely lilies.
    The friendly white doves wafting in the warm air
    Like angels through clear skies to a heavenly fair.
    And he, staring me silently with such bright eyes
    Melts my heart in gratitude as it heaves its sighs.

4. He paces through the garden as if in a hurry,
    Its residents greeting him with graceful curtsy.
    Had he and I but tried when he was yet alive,
    My love life would've had its place to thrive.
    Here, I forget all of love's ludicrous insanity;
    Solitude, conceit, deceit, and mundanity.

5. Goodbye lazy daisies, should be back tomorrow,
    If I live through the wrath and wallow in sorrow.
    You too, fluffy bunny; do not hide your head,
    Sad I'm leaving, I'd rather be right here instead.
    And he nods as the sun peeps through the dome,
    To say sorry, he couldn't be my partner at home.

69. THEIR LOVE, SPURIOUS AND PREMATURE

1. Once they asked how much he valued
      Their very odd menage,
   Not that his true comfort they cared,
      'Twas for their own image.

2. Sure, they would ask while on the train,
      Riding with souls well fed
   By him who must endure their pain
      Without a murmur said.

3. Often they come and closer still
      For nourishment and bread,
   With cries for him to foot the bill
      For their excessive spread.

4. When he declined to steer their train,
      Rebukes were vile and sure,
   Proving that sponges' love remain
      Spurious and premature.

70. THERE IS BEAUTY IN EVERYTHING

1. There is beauty in everything,
    If one could only see
   Past the ugly side of life, and
    Imagine what might be.

2. Some relations that rend apart
    When fret and fight prevail,
   Were once appealing partnerships
    Ere falling off the rail.

3. Wars have no regard for dear life,
    Its killings never cease.
   Oft, this carnage unveils to man
    The charm of ceaseless peace.

4. E'en death with morose in sorrow,
    Grants rest to weary souls.
   Though its survivors strain with pain,
    Souls make heav'n's honor rolls.

5. And those that may not be pleasing
    Much to our naked eyes,
   May burst with loving in their hearts
    That blesses binding ties.

6. There is beauty in everything
    Beyond whom plays the part.
   E'en neath a beast's fearsome façade
    Lies a good handsome heart.

71. TRUEST OF ALL ETERNAL SOULS

1. Truest of all eternal souls,
        She weathers every storm,
   With much precision marches on
        And to her beat conform.

2. She pauses not for anyone;
        Monarch, clergy, or throng,
   Yet, her paucity warrants they
        Keep marching right along.

3. Though faultless like the daily sun,
        Lagging or fast may look,
   And restless folk shrink in fear when
        Keeping up with her walk.

4. Some reminisce on those joyous,
        Dear rendezvous with her,
   While others curse, accuse her for
        Changing the way they were.

5. Mother to all eternal souls,
        She nurtures and makes plans;
   The sublime sun and earth and moon
        Step just as she aligns.

6. She marches on in steady steps,
        Knowing each one is tracked
   By countless counters all around,
        Precise as she has trekked.

72. TWO MEN WHO CHANGED THE WORLD

1. Two men were close to each other,
    Hand in hand, brother to brother,
        Whose friendship changed the world.
    Trekked breadth and length of Galilee
    And helped the lame, the blind to see;
        Compassion, they unfurled.

2. But one, to fraud he did subscribe,
    Plotted with heads and took a bribe,
        Betraying his dear friend.
    But soon was filled with great remorse,
    Returned the bribe too late, because
        Heaven, he did offend.

3. The other man condemned to die
    By those to whom he would not lie,
        Accused of high treason.
    Though not one fault in him was found,
    They beat and savaged, mocked, and bound,
        And hung for no reason.

4. Indeed, both men did hang to die,
    Yet one did rise to clouds on high,
        Enthroned with God in heav'n.
    He saved the lands from sin and stain,
    Eradicate their guilt and pain
        With all their sins forgiv'n.

5. The two men's lives did change the world,
    Yet, one was man, the other, God;
        The man took his own life.
    Our God gives life e'en to this day
    If man would worship him and say,
        I trust the God of life.

73. Upon a Mother

This tomb, a great life contains,
Lifeless, though are her remains.
Through her labors, a future
For many of her culture.
Rest, O queen of nurture, rest.
By your nature, souls are blest.

74. WALKING THE STREET

1. Walking the street, she was almost
        Hit by a moving entity,
   But was saved by a tumbling tree;
        It was sheer serendipity.

2. Playing numbers on the cop's car
        From the strange scene in the city,
   She won a game of chance that will
        Pay her in perpetuity.

3. She squandered some of her earnings
        And people showed her no pity,
   But scorned, railed, and disparaged her
        In noisy negativity.

4. With her wealth, he feigned love for her,
        Though he'd once ditched their amity.
   She could see through his deception
        With her pure perceptivity.

5. She gave the rest of her earnings
        To a budding kids' charity.
   This and other selfless deeds showed
        Her awesome authenticity.

6. When she passed, her gracious goodwill
        Displayed much durability,
   And partnered with other bequests
        To enhance frail humanity.

75. WATCHING A FATHER WITH HIS SON

1. Watching a father with his son
      Overwhelms my dear heart.
   Emotions such a sight evoke
      Ne'er from my mind depart.

2. Things he shares with his little lad;
      Like thrills from sports they see,
   A game of catch, fly-fishing trips
      And boating out at sea.

3. With Silverback-like instincts guides
      His son's every action;
   Protects from paths with perils fraught
      With wisdom and passion.

4. Foggy roots of held traditions
      Triggers their curious search;
   The passing of paternal torch,
      Olympia cannot match.

5. Watching a father with his son;
      Sad memories of my own,
   Who failed to care and share with me
      When he absconded town.

76. WHAT I'M I TO BELIEVE?

1.   I was thrilled when my wife
      Joined the posh pudding club;
    She ate of an amazing fruit
      That gave her core a stub.

2.   She claimed it was my plate
      From which she grabbed the fruit.
    I long had thought it was my friend's;
      A hunch, no proof to suit.

3.   And so, the wait was on,
      With months dragging to nine.
    Her stub progressed to swollen stump
      Exposing her waistline.

4.   Then came the dainty cub
      On a still summer's eve.
    With him quite smack of daddy's friend,
      What am I to believe?

77. WHILE ABOARD LIFE'S TRAIN

1. When I was young and heard them preach
   Of joyful sunny days ahead,
   Prayed I those days would swiftly reach
   Their radiant years instead.

2. But answered prayers were wanting;
   Supplanting our unworried ways
   Are hours of mourn for those moving
   Onward to cloudless days.

3. Just this summer, I held her hand,
   But she complained mine was quite cold,
   Then she succumbed and quickly joined
   The saints' immortal fold.

4. Then today, next door, the cold cook
   Arrived to claim another friend;
   Each day snatches its feeble folk
   As if life's now a fiend.

5. Perhaps time, I shouldn't presuppose,
   But savor daily those aboard
   Life's train in their joys and purpose,
   Before it runs aground.

78. WHO AM I?

1. My vast power derides the downtrodden,
   Whipping up strife and spreading hate
   On the weak whose fervor dissipate;
   To this belief, I'm beholden.
   Who am I, you ask?

2. I show great favor, only to my clan,
   Putting stumbling blocks on the poor;
   Pausing their paltry advancement plan,
   With tough laws and shutting the door.
   Some of what I do.

3. I proudly pervert justice oftentimes
   When it surges my grand power;
   Accuse falsely, the weak of my crimes,
   Stirring their lament and cower.
   This isn't all I do.

4. The weak, I remind of the whip and rope,
   Because they tremble at this trope.
   Grant them a piece, every now and then,
   Casting them callous to their pain.
   This is what I do.

5. I ne'er look the part, but e'en if I could,
   Won't tell the story of my heart.
   I'm from a proud biased brotherhood,
   Privileged, though I'm not that smart.
   Yes, I am this too.

6. Yet, within my heart, much doubtful and scared,
   Pond 'ring how long my act would last.
   If they had a chance, would I be spared,
   Forgiv'n, or would they have a blast
   With me, the victim?

79. WORLD'S DAMNING SILENCE

1. Hard to imagine that she did
        Play dead while tyrants reigned;
    Amidst their terror, blight, and gore,
        Concern she mostly feigned.

2. The helpless Jews suffered abuse
        From Fuhrer's furious force;
    Six million and more perished souls,
        She could have spared from worse.

3. Slavery much darkness had imposed
        On the dark skinned of man.
    Her carnal patrons profited
        From her hush on their plan.

4. Apartheid showed that she had gained
        No courage from her past;
    Her spineless actions did ensure
        Its damning impacts last.

5. Shame on her silence and consent
        For helpless souls' defeat.
    Her reckless errors of the past,
        She must never repeat.

80. YOUR GRACE

1. My whole life you have granted,
   My intellect you planted,
   Played part in acts unwanted,
   Yet, when my life was blasted,
   Your hand was always near.

2. Your love, I've been receiving,
   Since early days of living
   Yet oft my mind is waffling,
   And when my life is drifting,
   I find your spirit near.

3. My food you've been providing
   From your grace quite abounding,
   Yet, my mouth is still wanting
   And when my mind is doubting,
   I can yet hear you there.

4. I take your grace for granted,
   Your pow'r I oft discounted
   And do things you detested,
   But, when I am left stranded,
   I can yet find you near.

5. My past sins notwithstanding,
   Your promise not discerning,
   Your grace always abounding
   And when my life is ending,
   I will yet find you there.

LIMERICKS

1. Ate Escargot

Said he'd eat things to make his car go.
"Think of something that goes with cargo",
Said his sly brother,
Tired of his bother.
Hence, he ate the slimy escargot.

2. Fete in the Hall

We were at a fete in the hall
Dancing and having quite a ball.
But she had the gall
To make the wrong call
And have music stopped in the hall.

3. Girl Who Found a Cent

There was a girl who found a cent
In the stairwell on her descent.
Then she gave her cent
To her mum who'd sent
Her on the steep stairwell ascent.

4. Happy When He Can Dance

He's much happy when he can dance,
Then dances when he has the chance.
Without any chance
To be at a dance,
He's unhappy since he can't dance.

5. HE USED A CANDLE

In the dark, he used a candle
To write sweet music like Handel.
Absent the candle,
He was unable
To write sweet music like Handel.

6. HIS DEAR WAS THERE

The only one there was his dear;
No one else dared to be near there.
For out of much fear,
Of the wild lion near,
The only one there was his dear.

7. HIS HOUSE

His house was full of wine and gold,
His wealth much more than kings could hold,
But the day he died,
No one really cared,
But for the plenty wine and gold.

8. I CARE NOT FOR THE BEAR

I swear, I care not for the bear
Whose rare stare made me spill the beer.
He gave me a scare,
When he shared a stare;
The bear's stare made me spill the beer.

9. I Owe Her

Said where she's from, grows lots of corn,
Oft is cold but is lots of fun.
I lost the wager,
When I couldn't name where;
Therefore, now sadly Iowa.

10. Man from Beech

There's a man from Beech named John Goodson
With a son whose name was Jack Goodson.
When father and son
Engaged in arson,
The Goodsons of Beech went to prison.

11. Man from Havre de Grace

There was a man from Havre de Grace
Who sought his bad repute erase,
But could not confess,
And would not redress,
Because he did not have the grace.

12. My Fine, Young Lad

My fine young lad was a tad sad,
Said a dad who recently had
To see just how bad,
A sad day he had,
When his mad hound died on his pad.

13. Naughty and Haughty

He was naughty when he drank hot tea
And being naughty makes him quite haughty.
Naughty makes him bad,
Haughty makes him proud.
He should never think to drink hot tea.

14. Peeping Tom

Was known by his given name, Tom
As in, not yet a peeping Tom,
But after he peeped
At the woman stripped,
He soon became a peeping Tom.

15. Performed to Much Acclaim

Said she performed to much acclaim
Yet, no one then could back her claim.
But the kid confirmed
That she had performed,
Just not as she'd said in her claim.

16. Pot of Gold

Her heart was like a pot of gold.
Moreover, she was hot and bold.
And then I was told,
Even when it's cold,
She's hotter than hot pot of gold.

17. SATAN, THE DISCIPLE

Eve approached Adam, her dear man
And told him someone said, he can
Eat of the apple
Like the disciple.
Turns out disciple was Satan.

18. SET TO GET MICHELLE OUT

They were set to get Michelle out,
Because she wanted me shell out
Funds for a project,
Declared a reject
By those set to get Michelle out.

19. SHE LOVES ME

She loves me like she did before
But I thought what could that be for?
Then said she, how much,
She's touched by my touch
And loves me like she did before.

20. SHE SAID BYE-BYE

He stood by as she said bye-bye,
Then closed his eyes and heaved a sigh.
For she'd breathed her last,
Then quite quickly passed.
He'd thought, "what a way to bye-bye".

21. THE GOOD LIE

Father said, oft they the good, lie,
For they have to tell "the good lie".
What their minds do share,
Oft depends on where
Their sensed virtues of the good lie.

22. THE SHARP SHOOTER

Sherman says he's a sharp shooter,
And has made grand plans to shoot her.
But when he met her
In bar to shoot her,
Each had a shot; he couldn't shoot her.

23. THE TRANSFORMER

"I change ex-wives to pets like a transformer"
Said the man to him who would like his former
Wife to be his pets,
At first chance he gets.
Hence, he humbly asked the man to transform her.

24. WALK ALONG THE SEINE (RIVER IN FRANCE)

Said he had walked along the Seine.
She asked how he knew they're the sane.
He said, he didn't check
Whose mind wasn't a wreck,
But took a walk along the Seine.

Printed in the United States
by Baker & Taylor Publisher Services